Name: ______________________

Address: ______________________

____

____

Date of birth: ______________________

Nationality: ______________________

Height: ______________________

Eye colour: ______________________

Distinguishing characteristics: ______________________

____

____

____

Current photograph:

AF583585

Progressive speed trials

Copy this text into the lines below. Have a classmate time you. Then assess the fluency and legibility of your writing.

Date _ /_ /_ Time taken: __ seconds

The world contains amazing things — landforms and structures that have to be seen to be believed!

Rate your fluency.

Date _ /_ /_ Time taken: __ seconds

The world contains amazing things — landforms and structures that have to be seen to be believed!

Rate your fluency.

Date _ /_ /_ Time taken: __ seconds

The world contains amazing things — landforms and structures that have to be seen to be believed!

Rate your fluency.

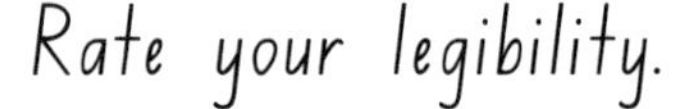

When you or your teacher notice any personalised element in your writing (for example, a letter or join that is different to ordinary Foundation cursive), record it on this page. If it doesn't slow you down or make your writing less legible, and you like it, stick with it. If not, think about how you could modify it.

HAPPY ALTERNATIVE

Date	Element of personal style	Is it useful?	If not, how would you like to modify it?	Practise the modified version here

☆ Revision – Letter formation

Date ___/___/___

Copy. Remember to include exit and/or entry flicks for the lower-case letters.

A a B b C c D d E e F f G g

H h I i J j K k L l M m

N n O o P p Q q R r S s T t

U u V v W w X x Y y Z z

Copy.

abcdefghijklmnopqrstuvwxyz abcdefghijklmnopqrstuvwxyz

Get ready to explore the wonders of the world!

1 2 3 4 5 6 7 8 9 10 20 30 40 50

Date ___ / ___ / ___

☆ Revision – Diagonal joins

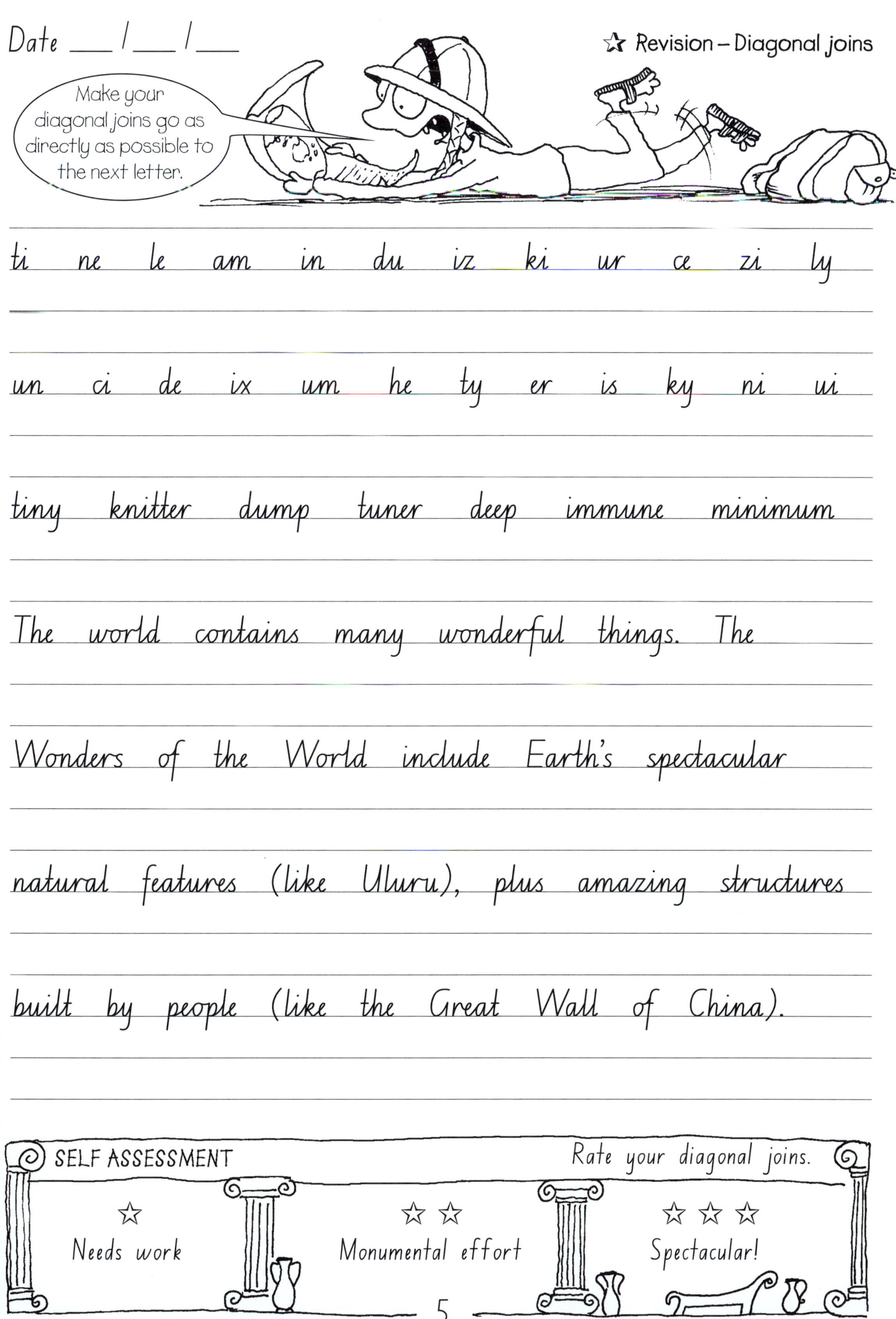

ti ne le am in du iz ki ur ce zi ly

un ci de ix um he ty er is ky ni ui

tiny knitter dump tuner deep immune minimum

The world contains many wonderful things. The

Wonders of the World include Earth's spectacular

natural features (like Uluru), plus amazing structures

built by people (like the Great Wall of China).

SELF ASSESSMENT

Rate your diagonal joins.

☆	☆☆	☆☆☆
Needs work	Monumental effort	Spectacular!

Date ___ / ___ / ___

el retrace nk retrace

th it ck nk ab nt tl et ht lt

title element mink keel untimely little minty

think clunky leek likely climb mutt imminent

The Great Pyramid at Giza is the only one of the Seven Wonders of the Ancient World that is still standing today.

SELF ASSESSMENT

Circle your best diagonal join to a head and body letter.

Date ___ / ___ / ___

ed ng lo ca if nd no dg ic to

elf noun cattle under click hedge clear

aqua land nudge danger half tangy nothing

The Hanging Gardens of Babylon were said to have

been built by King Nebuchadnezzar II for his wife,

Amytis, to remind her of home.

SELF ASSESSMENT

Rate your drop-in joins.

☆ Needs work

☆☆ Monumental effort

☆☆☆ Spectacular!

Date ___ / ___ / ___

on rn vi wn xi ru fi rm ou wi

vital monkey loud yawning fiery exit ooze

wiry armour onion roar vicious furry worm

The statue of Zeus at Olympia contained over a tonne of gold. It also contained ivory from elephants' tusks and hippopotamuses' teeth.

SELF ASSESSMENT

Underline your three best horizontal joins.

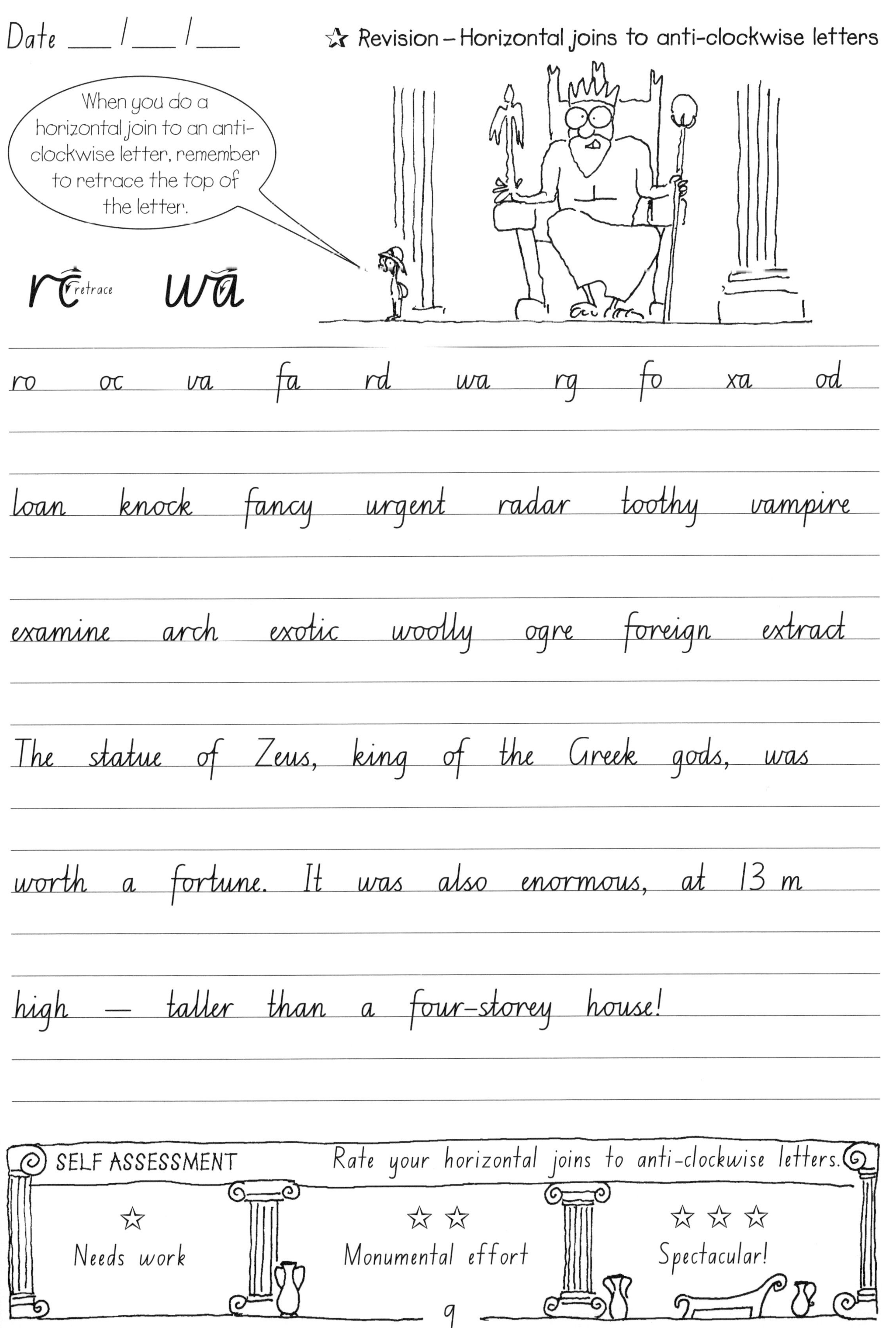

Date ___ / ___ / ___

☆ Revision – Horizontal joins to anti-clockwise letters

ro oc va fa rd wa rg fo xa od

loan knock fancy urgent radar toothy vampire

examine arch exotic woolly ogre foreign extract

The statue of Zeus, king of the Greek gods, was worth a fortune. It was also enormous, at 13 m high — taller than a four-storey house!

SELF ASSESSMENT Rate your horizontal joins to anti-clockwise letters.

☆	☆ ☆	☆ ☆ ☆
Needs work	Monumental effort	Spectacular!

Date ___ / ___ / ___

When you do a horizontal join to a tall letter, go right to the top, then retrace a bit as you come back down.

ot (retrace) fl (retrace)

wh of rl ot fl rt rf ok wl xt

extreme newt roof where hook flinch owl

bawl lark party garland follow surf exhibit

The Colossus of Rhodes was an extremely big statue.

It was said a person's arms could not reach

around one of the statue's fingers.

SELF ASSESSMENT

Circle the word with the best horizontal join to a tall letter.

Date ___ /___ /___

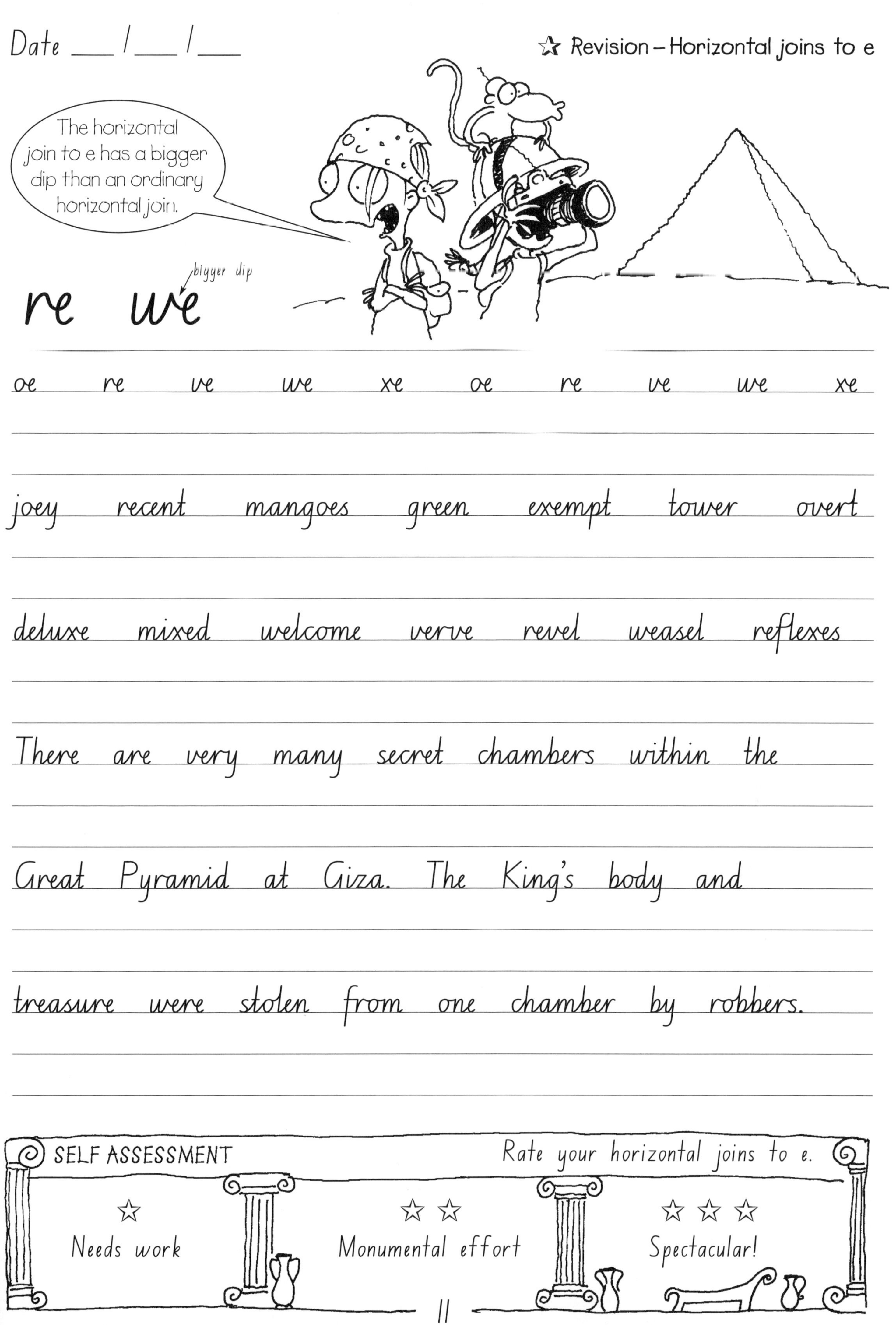

oe re ve we xe oe re ve we xe

joey recent mangoes green exempt tower overt

deluxe mixed welcome verve revel weasel reflexes

There are very many secret chambers within the

Great Pyramid at Giza. The King's body and

treasure were stolen from one chamber by robbers.

SELF ASSESSMENT Rate your horizontal joins to e.

☆	☆☆	☆☆☆
Needs work	Monumental effort	Spectacular!

Date ___ / ___ / ___

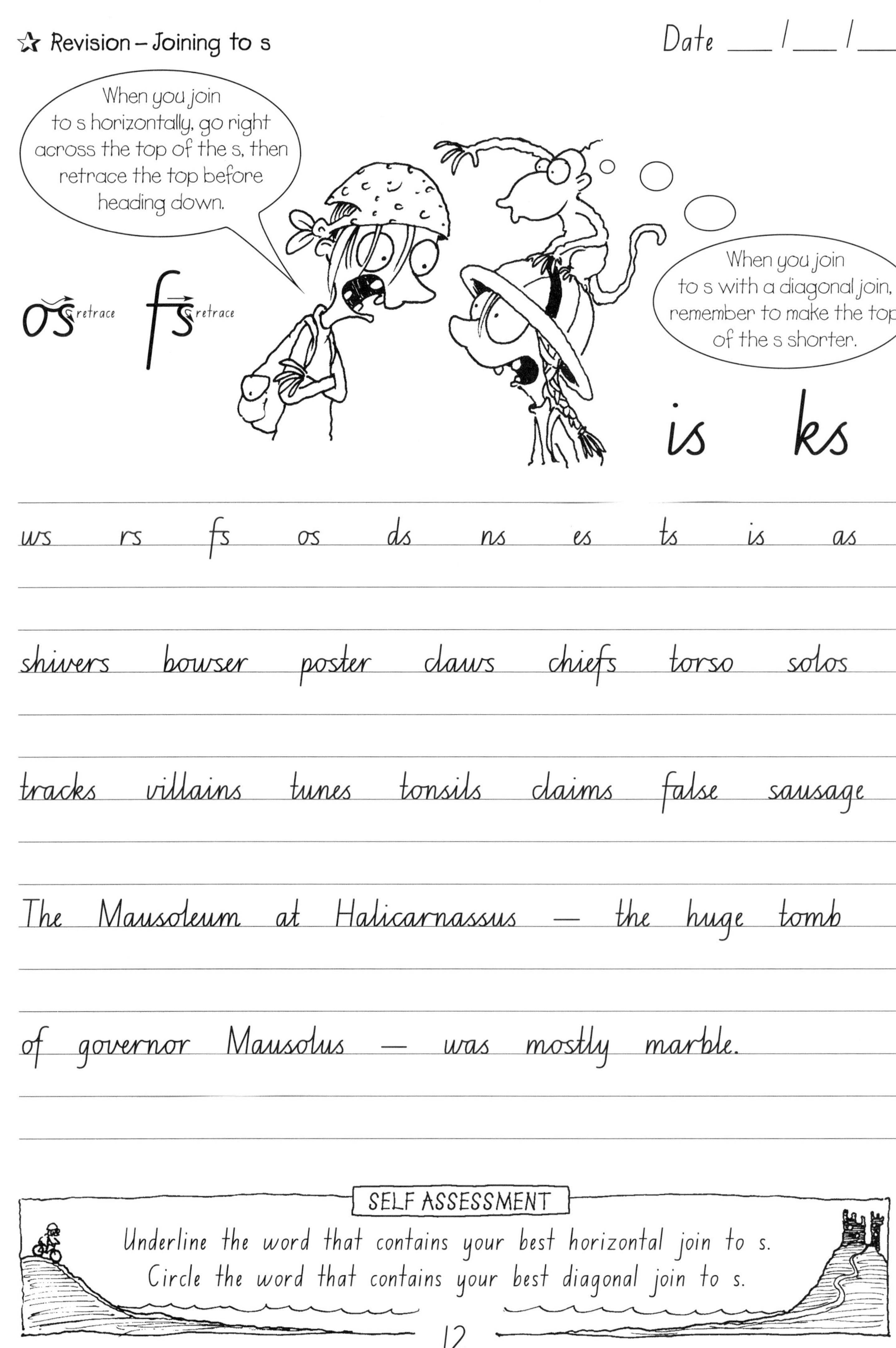

ws rs fs os ds ns es ts is as

shivers bowser poster claws chiefs torso solos

tracks villains tunes tonsils claims false sausage

The Mausoleum at Halicarnassus — the huge tomb

of governor Mausolus — was mostly marble.

SELF ASSESSMENT

Underline the word that contains your best horizontal join to s.
Circle the word that contains your best diagonal join to s.

Date ___ / ___ / ___
It's quickest to join double f with one crossbar. You can go on to join from the crossbar as you would with a single f.
office ruffle
ff ff ff ff ff ff ff ff ff ff
scuff sniff bluff cliff baffle daffodil traffic
effigy stuffing raffish truffle effort puffy muffler
The Pharos at Alexandria was a terrifically tall
lighthouse that burned wood to afford light. It was
effective — it could be seen 55 km off.
SELF ASSESSMENT
Rate your joined double f's.
☆
Needs work
☆ ☆
Monumental effort
☆ ☆ ☆
Spectacular!

☆ Revision – Joining f and t

Date ___ / ___ / ___

ft ft ft ft ft ft ft ft ft ft

rift after often deftly sifting nifty hovercraft

shift draft fifth lofty swiftly soften weightlifter

The Pharos at Alexandria was built soon after 300 BC, and remains the tallest lighthouse ever made. Shifts of horses hefted fuel to the top.

SELF ASSESSMENT

Circle your best joined ft.

Date ___ / ___ / ___

☆ Revision – Fluency joins from b, p, s

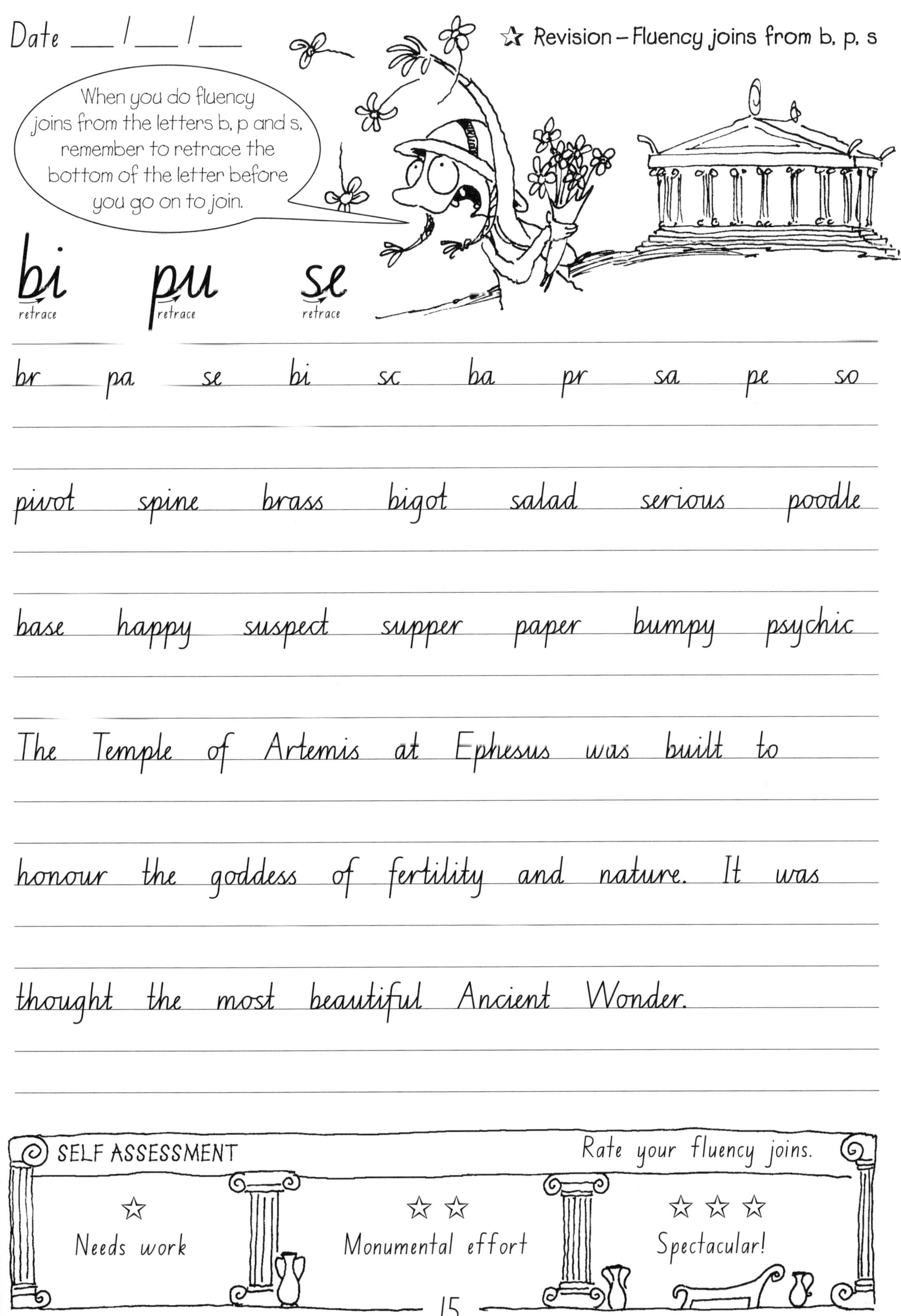

br pa se bi sc ba pr sa pe so

pivot spine brass bigot salad serious poodle

base happy suspect supper paper bumpy psychic

The Temple of Artemis at Ephesus was built to

honour the goddess of fertility and nature. It was

thought the most beautiful Ancient Wonder.

SELF ASSESSMENT

Rate your fluency joins.

☆	☆ ☆	☆ ☆ ☆
Needs work	Monumental effort	Spectacular!

☆ Revision – Fluency joins to head and body letters

Date ___ / ___ / ___

When you do a fluency join to a head and body letter, go right to the top of the letter, then retrace a bit on your way back down.

sh (retrace) bl (retrace) pt (retrace)

sh bl pt st pl sl sk ph sh pl

shonky pleated skittle blood stretch phoney doubt

cash obtain risky cipher aisle supple asteroid

blast apple abrupt doubter strain slushy rubbish

Many master sculptors worked on the Temple at

Ephesus, carving life-sized figures in the marble.

SELF ASSESSMENT

Circle your three best fluency joins to a head and body letter.

Date ___ /___ /___

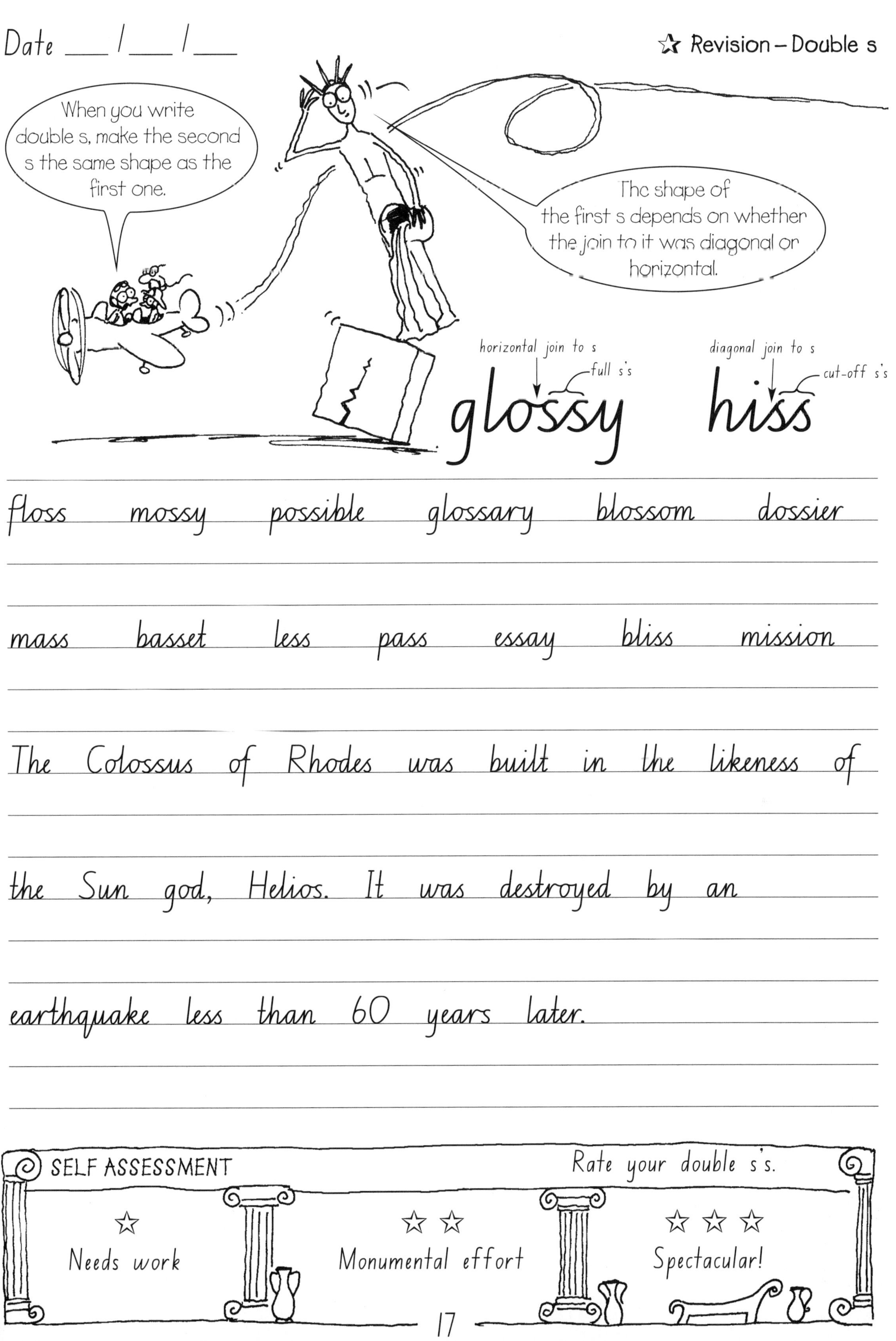

floss mossy possible glossary blossom dossier

mass basset less pass essay bliss mission

The Colossus of Rhodes was built in the likeness of the Sun god, Helios. It was destroyed by an earthquake less than 60 years later.

SELF ASSESSMENT — Rate your double s's.

☆	☆ ☆	☆ ☆ ☆
Needs work	Monumental effort	Spectacular!

Assessment page – Joins

Date ___ / ___ / ___

Write each word in cursive.

Diagonal joins

link funky lemur unlikely destiny clump muzzle

Drop-in joins

under mince unfair candle magnify aquatic delicacy

Horizontal joins

flexible moon horizon honey whip flavour argue

Horizontal joins to e

weekly event ferret mixer twenty awesome dominoes

Joining to s

terse news crispy monsters floss messy bossiness

Double f and joined ft

whiff buffet raffle effort lift hefty camshaft

Fluency joins

purple scabby blister shaky pester spring surprise

Teacher

Date ___ / ___ / ___

Speed test

Read the sentence below, and memorise it if you can. Write out the sentence as many times as you can in 2 minutes. Have a classmate time you.

There were many other wonders in the Ancient World besides those included in the familiar list of seven.

Total number of words: ______ Divide by two for speed in words per minute: ______

SELF ASSESSMENT

Rate your fluency.

☆ ☆☆ ☆☆☆

Rate your legibility.

☆ ☆☆ ☆☆☆

Speed loops from body and tail letters – g, j, y

Date ___ /___ /___

You can join from the tails of g, j and y, using speed loops.

Remember that speed loops from body and tail letters should cross at the baseline.

gi jo ye

speed loops from tails cross at the baseline

ghost gory gruesome greasy gristle glamour glisten

jealous jeans jigsaw joking jacket juicy jugular

yam yearn young yesterday yummy yellow yacht

igloo rajah playing haggle injure ogre yoyo

Use four of these words in a sentence, using speed loops.

SELF ASSESSMENT

Circle the words that contain

- the best speed loop from g
- the best speed loop from j
- the best speed loop from y.

Date ___ /___ /___
To use speed loops from z, you need to learn a new z shape. This z has a tail. Join from the tail the same way you would from g, j and y.
z becomes ʒ
lazy
When the z is at the end of the word, you don't need the loop because it's not going to join to anything.
buzz
no loop at end of word
zip zap zoo zero zing zebra zig-zag
hazy size maze doze froze crazy brazen
hazard breeze razor dozen azure hazel amazing
buzzard dizzy fuzzy pizza buzz jazz pizzazz
SELF ASSESSMENT
Rate your speed loops from z.
☆ Needs work
☆☆ Monumental effort
☆☆☆ Spectacular!

Date ___ /___ /___

The Ancient Egyptians weren't the only ones to build pyramids. The Aztecs also built them – the Great Temple of Tenochtitlán, for example. Although only a fifth as tall as the Great Pyramid at Giza, this amazing structure was still an impressive size, being 30 metres high. One of the two temples at the top was dedicated to Huitzilopochtli, the god of the Sun and of war.

SELF ASSESSMENT

Use a highlighter pen to highlight the line with the best speed loops from z.

Date ___ /___ /___

Remember to keep your speed loops quite narrow – otherwise they can slow you down!

al th lb nk

slink towel reach brisk smash total bulb

cheat elbow thank masked absorb thumb rabble

One of the wonders of the modern world is the Channel Tunnel that links Great Britain and France. The main tunnels lie about 45 m beneath the seabed of the English Channel.

SELF ASSESSMENT Rate your speed loops to head and body letters.

☆ Needs work

☆☆ Monumental effort

☆☆☆ Spectacular!

Date ___ /___ /___

You can join **from** f with a speed loop. You can also join **to** f with a speed loop.

The only time you need to use a crossbar with a speed loop f is when it comes at the end of a word.

first affect self

fantastic free furry features fickle fleapit force

sofa chafe rifle strife spiffy toffee snuffle

clef chief serif sniff chaff bailiff flagstaff

The Eiffel Tower in Paris, France, is one of the

world's most famous landmarks.

SELF ASSESSMENT

Circle the words with

- the best speed loop f at the beginning of a word
- the best speed loop f in the middle of a word
- the best speed loop f at the end of a word.

Date ___ / ___ / ___

Remember, speed loops are optional. Use them if they help you to write faster and more fluently.

The Statue of Liberty was a gift from the people of France to the people of the United States. It is a symbol of international friendship, freedom and democracy. The statue is made of 91 tonnes of copper sheets over a huge iron framework. The framework was designed by Gustave Eiffel. The sculptor, Frédéric-Auguste Bartholdi, modelled the statue on his mother.

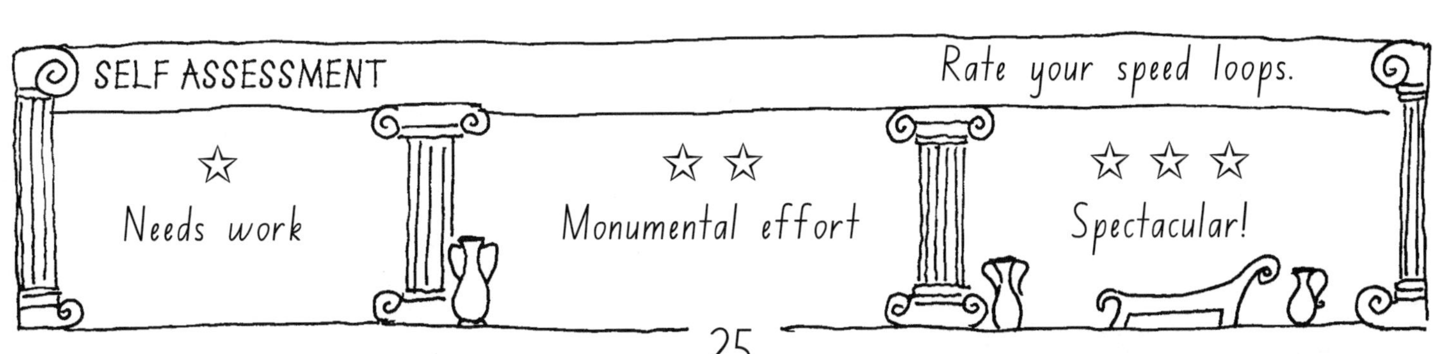

Date ___ / ___ / ___

Copy, adding in the speed loops.

gross adjacent yeast enjoying amaze snazzy fizz

startle thing awake ruby chips smelly ankle

fringe feasting influence trifle sniffle chef stuff

jelly jewels gleaming beagle royal flamboyant zebra

Rewrite this passage in cursive script with speed loops.

The Statue of Liberty was built in France, then shipped to the United States in 350 pieces. It took just four months to reassemble it. The statue's nose is 1.48 m long. The seven rays of the crown represent the seven seas and continents of the world.

Teacher

Date ___ / ___ / ___

Speed test

Look at the sentence and memorise it if you can. Copy it as many times as you can in 1 minute, using speed loops. Have a classmate time you. Then rate your legibility.

> The Alhambra in Spain is a beautiful palace that includes a fortress, courtyards, gardens and fountains.

Number of words ___ Legibility ☆ ☆☆ ☆☆☆

Now try it **without** using speed loops. Again, have a classmate time you.

Number of words ___ Legibility ☆ ☆☆ ☆☆☆

Was your writing faster with or without speed loops? ________

Was your writing more legible with or without speed loops? ________

Date ___ / ___ / ___

Keeping your letters an even size will help increase your fluency.

Alhambra
uneven letter size

Alhambra
even letter size

The Leaning Tower of Pisa is the bell tower of the cathedral in Pisa, Italy. It was begun in 1173. By 1178, with just three of its eight storeys built, the lean became obvious. The Tower leans to the south because the foundations on that side are sinking into the soft soil. By 1990, it was leaning so far over that it was in danger of falling, and was closed to tourists.

Copy. Choose one line of text, and rule a line straight across at the level of the tallest head and body letter. Then rule another line across at the level of the tallest body letter.

SELF ASSESSMENT

Tick the line that has the most consistent letter size.

Even letter spacing makes writing easier to read. Copy the text then test your letter spacing by choosing one line and writing a dot at each point where your letters touch the baseline.

Leaning Leaning
uneven letter spacing even letter spacing

In 1999, engineers made another attempt to fix the

Leaning Tower of Pisa. This time they carefully took

soil out from under the north side of the Tower. It

worked! The Tower is now a bit straighter and more

stable, and should be safe for at least 200 years.

SELF ASSESSMENT Rate your letter spacing.

☆	☆☆	☆☆☆
Needs work	Monumental effort	Spectacular!

Date ___ /___ /___

Spacing your words evenly will make your writing more legible. Copy the text, then choose a line, and test your word spacing by writing the letter o in between each word.

The o ten o chapels o have o colourful o domes. ← good spacing

The ten chapels have colourful domes. ← o's won't fit between words

The o ten o chapels o have o colourful o domes. ↖ too spacy

St Basil's Cathedral in Moscow was built in the

1550s on the orders of Tsar Ivan IV, also known

as "Ivan the Terrible". It contains ten chapels topped

with colourful, patterned domes. The onion shape of

the domes stops the roofs collapsing under heavy snow.

SELF ASSESSMENT

Use a highlighter pen to highlight the line with the best word spacing.

Date ___ /___ /___

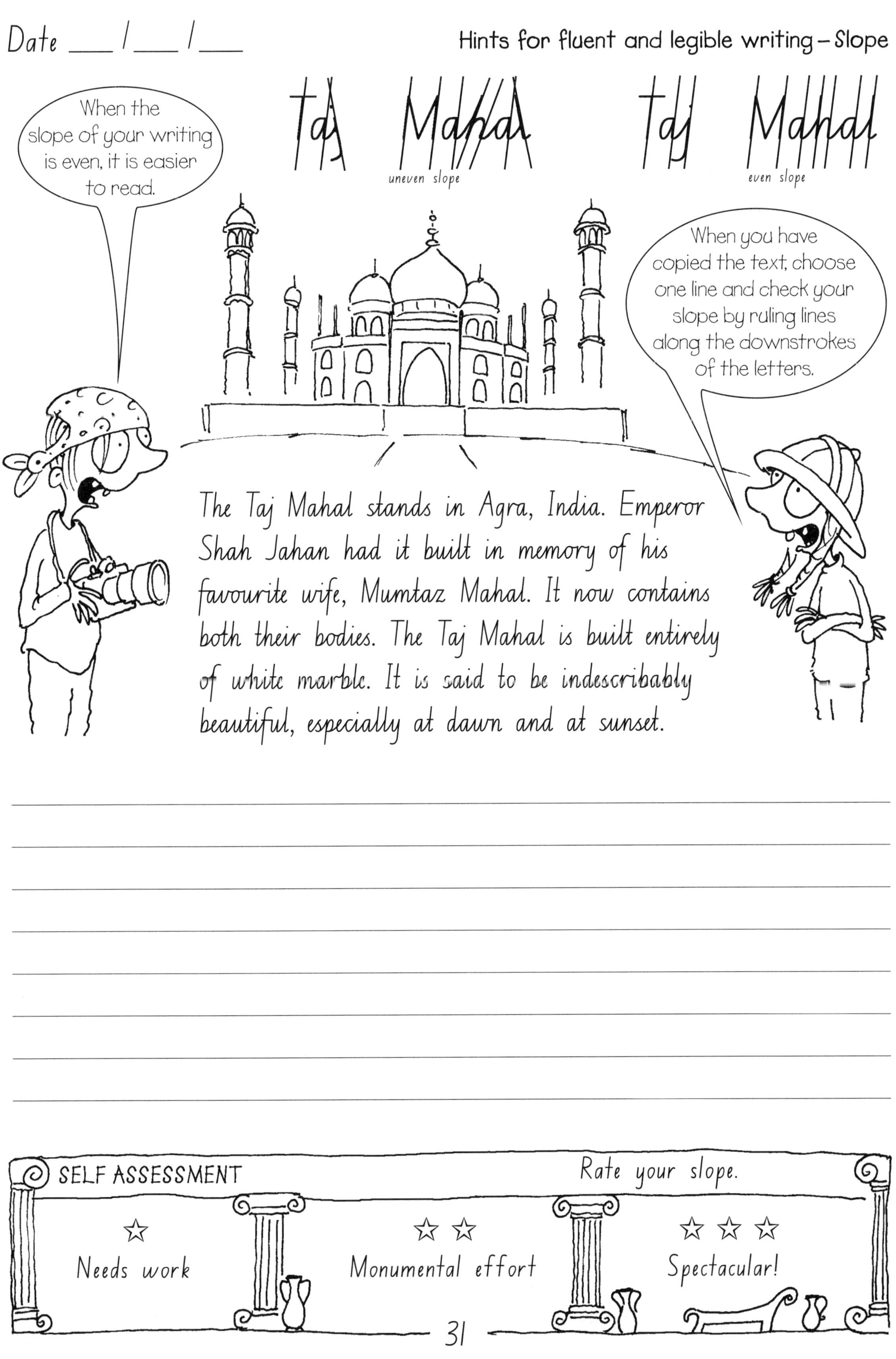

The Taj Mahal stands in Agra, India. Emperor Shah Jahan had it built in memory of his favourite wife, Mumtaz Mahal. It now contains both their bodies. The Taj Mahal is built entirely of white marble. It is said to be indescribably beautiful, especially at dawn and at sunset.

SELF ASSESSMENT — Rate your slope.

☆	☆ ☆	☆ ☆ ☆
Needs work	Monumental effort	Spectacular!

Date ___ /___ /___

Pencil lifts, like at drop-in joins, give your hand a break. They also give you a chance to move your hand across the page.

Move your hand and arm across together – don't bend your hand back at the wrist.

Choose one line and make a mark like this ′ above each place you will lift your pencil. Then copy.

Before the Panama Canal was built, ships had to

sail right around the bottom of South America to

travel between the Atlantic and Pacific Oceans. The

82 km Canal can cut travelling distances by up to

12,875 km! It cut sailing times from roughly six

months to six weeks.

SELF ASSESSMENT

Do your hand and arm move across together?

Yes No Sometimes

Diagonal joins are the most common kind of join. To make your writing faster and smoother, make your diagonal joins go as directly as possible to the next letter.

Stone circles such as Stonehenge may have been burial places, as well as being used for astronomical calculations. One of the weirder wonders of the world is Carhenge, in Nebraska, U.S.. It's a copy of Stonehenge made from old cars. Jim Reinders, a farmer and artist, built Carhenge as a memorial to his dead father.

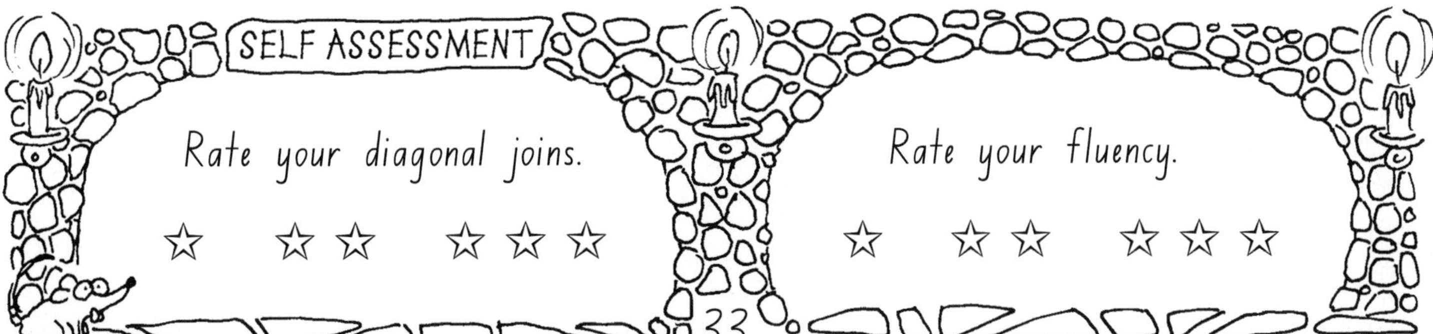

Date ___ / ___ / ___

To make your writing more legible, make sure each dropped-in letter touches the exit flick before it.

One day in 1938, a fisherman near Madagascar caught a strange fish. A visiting scientist spotted the fish, which was found to be a coelacanth. These large fish have heavy, dull blue scales and lobed fins — and were thought to have been extinct for 70 million years! Finding one was like "finding a live dinosaur roaming the earth".

SELF ASSESSMENT

Rate your drop-in joins.

☆ ☆☆ ☆☆☆

Rate your letter spacing.

☆ ☆☆ ☆☆☆

Date ___ / ___ / ___

Your writing will be more legible if the horizontal joins from o, r, v, w and x have just a small dip. The horizontal join from f is straight.

The Grand Canyon in Arizona, U.S., is one of the most spectacular of the world's natural wonders. It's unbelievably enormous – 1.6 km deep and 15 km wide. It has taken millions of years for the Colorado River to gouge out this huge channel. In the process, many layers of rock have been exposed. The layers are in striking colours, and these colours change with the light and the season.

SELF ASSESSMENT

Rate your horizontal joins.

☆ ☆☆ ☆☆☆

Rate your word spacing.

☆ ☆☆ ☆☆☆

 Date ___ / ___ / ___

Horizontal joins to e have a slightly bigger dip than ordinary horizontal joins. But don't make them too dippy, or they'll slow you down.

shoelace oboe foes phoenix whoever vetoed shoes

tattooed poet desperadoes echoed toenail manoeuvre

The Great Barrier Reef is the world's largest coral reef. It is more than 2,000 km long and is forever growing. It features an awesome variety of sea creatures and multi-coloured corals.

SELF ASSESSMENT

Rate your horizontal joins to e.

☆ ☆☆ ☆☆☆

Rate your slope.

☆ ☆☆ ☆☆☆

Date ___ / ___ / ___

Remember to retrace the top of the s after a horizontal join, and to use the cut-off s after a diagonal join.

Kakadu National Park is a vast wilderness. Much

of the land belongs to the Gagudju people, who

have lived there for over 40,000 years. Kakadu's

landscape features cliffs, ravines and waterfalls, as

well as grasslands, forests, swamps and rivers. If

you visit, beware of the saltwater crocodiles — they'll

attack anything that comes too close!

SELF ASSESSMENT

Rate your joins to s.

☆ ☆☆ ☆☆☆

Rate your fluency.

☆ ☆☆ ☆☆☆

 Date ___ /___ /___

When you write double f, you can go on to join from the crossbar as you would from the crossbar of a single f.

But when you join ft, go on to join from the exit flick of the t, then come back and do the crossbar last.

join from crossbar

fluffy

do crossbar last

deftly

join from exit flick of t

Another rather different wonder is the world's largest collection of navel fluff. Since 1984, Australia's Graham Barker has managed to deftly collect 15.41 g of his own navel fluff. While some may scoff, or find collecting navel fluff a daft hobby, for Graham it's just part of his daily routine. Graham's goal is to gather enough of the soft fluff to stuff a cushion.

SELF ASSESSMENT

Circle your best joined double f and your best joined ft.
Tick the line that has the most consistent slope.

Date ___ / ___ / ___

Fluency joins from the letters b, p and s will help you write faster and more smoothly.

blazing party sandwich break peach skin parcel

slippery pudding bumps soapy babble deepest spring

The Galapagos Islands are found in the eastern Pacific Ocean. They are famous for their beauty, and for the variety and uniqueness of the plants and animals there. Some species are only ever found on specific islands in this group.

SELF ASSESSMENT

Rate your fluency joins.

☆ ☆☆ ☆☆☆

Rate your letter and word spacing.

☆ ☆☆ ☆☆☆

Date ___ / ___ / ___

If you use speed loops, keep them quite narrow. Speed loops that are too wide can slow you down!

yelling juicy grateful zeal spiffy rabid chalk

Kata Tjuta is a group of roughly 30 rounded rock domes that lies just 24 km to the west of Uluru, in central Australia. This amazing rock formation is also known as the Olgas. Kata Tjuta has great importance in Aboriginal culture. At sunset, the domes glow luminous orange.

SELF ASSESSMENT

Rate your speed loops.

☆ ☆☆ ☆☆☆

Rate your fluency.

☆ ☆☆ ☆☆☆

Where would you find thousands of limestone pillars standing in a desert? The answer is: in Western Australia! The Pinnacles are an extraordinary sight – every one is different. Some are the size of cars, and others are the size of your little finger. They are also all kinds of shapes, and some have been given names like "Camel", "Kangaroo" and "Molars".

SELF ASSESSMENT

Rate your punctuation.

☆ ☆☆ ☆☆☆

Rate your legibility.

☆ ☆☆ ☆☆☆

Date ___ /___ /___

When you're taking notes, you don't want your writing to be fancy – just fast! But you need it to be legible, so that when you go back you can read what you wrote.

Write this sentence out as many times as you can in a minute. Have a classmate time you.

Australia contains some of the most breathtaking natural wonders in the world.

Number of words ______ Legibility ☆ ☆☆ ☆☆☆

Sloping your writing a little bit more, while still keeping the slope even, can help you write faster. So can spacing your words out a bit more.

Copy the sentence again as many times as you can in a minute. This time slope your writing a little more, and leave a little more space between words.

Number of words ______ Legibility ☆ ☆☆ ☆☆☆

Date ___ /___ /___

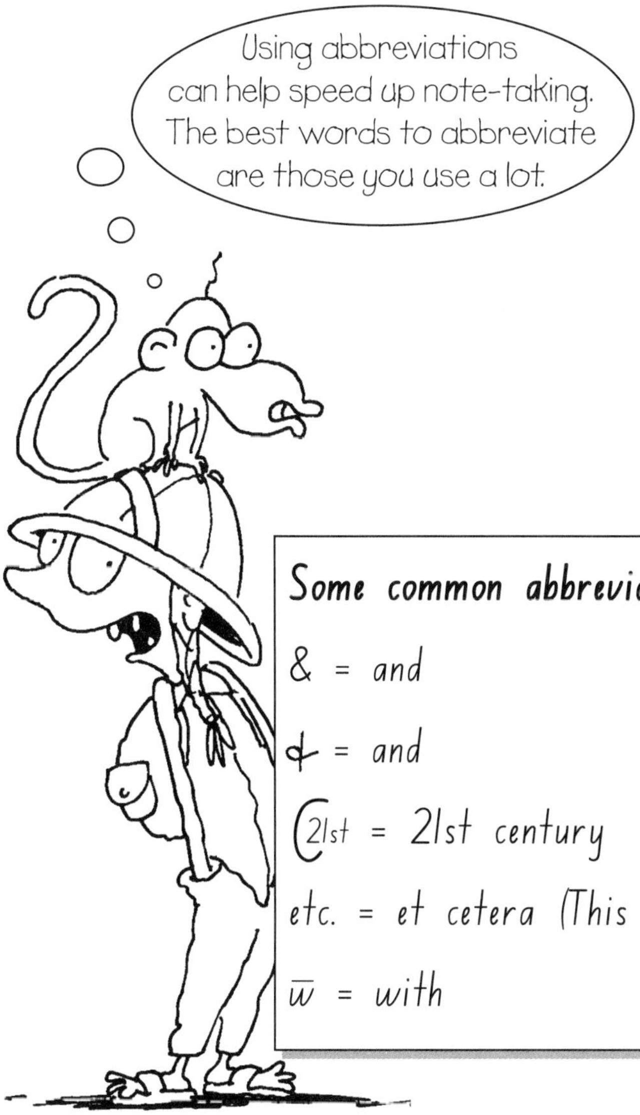

Using abbreviations can help speed up note-taking. The best words to abbreviate are those you use a lot.

The important thing is to find abbreviations that work for you, and then stick with them. If you vary them, you may not remember what you meant.

Some common abbreviations:

& = and

+ = and

C21st = 21st century

etc. = et cetera (This means "and other things".)

w̄ = with

List some words you think it might be useful to abbreviate. Try out some abbreviations for them.

Which abbreviations would you like to experiment with some more?

Assessment page – Fluency and legibility

Date ___ / ___ / ___

Write this passage out in cursive. Then:

- ☆ choose one line and add a dot at each point where your writing touches the baseline
- ☆ choose another line and write an o between each word
- ☆ choose another line and rule lines along the downstrokes.

Keli Mutu lies on the island of Flores in Indonesia. The volcano at Keli Mutu is still active, and three lakes fill its three craters. The amazing thing about them is that each lake is a different colour. One of the lakes was originally a rich glowing red, but has got gradually darker and is now almost black. The lake next to it is an opaque emerald green. The third lake is a transparent sparkling green.

Teacher

Date ___ / ___ / ___

Speed test

Read the sentence below, and memorise it if you can. Write out the sentence as many times as you can in 2 minutes. (Use speed loops if you want to.) Have a classmate time you.

A platypus is a natural wonder — a cat-sized egg-laying mammal with fur like a beaver, a duck's bill and webbed feet!

Number of words: ________

Divide by two for speed in words per minute: ________

SELF ASSESSMENT

Rate your fluency.

☆ ☆☆ ☆☆☆

Rate your legibility.

☆ ☆☆ ☆☆☆

You can repeat this test on another sheet at a later date to see if your speed's increased. Remember to assess your legibility as well. Speed means nothing if you can't read the writing!

Developing your own style – Double t with one crossbar Date ___ /___ /___

A speedy alternative to crossing the t's in tt separately is to cross them with one crossbar.

come back and do the crossbar last

tt attack

tt tt tt tt tt tt tt tt tt tt

attack little batting kitten letter bottom cottage

The Matterhorn is a spectacular mountain on the Italian-Swiss border. Herman Perren, from nearby Zermatt, wanted to climb it 150 times, but died on a climb less than 10 climbs short of his goal.

SELF ASSESSMENT Rate your double t's with one crossbar.

☆ Needs work

☆☆ Monumental effort

☆☆☆ Spectacular!

Date ___ /___ /___

You can join from the crossbar of t the same way you'd join from the crossbar of f. Notice that the t doesn't need an exit flick.

ti ta

ta ti to tu th tt tr ts tw ty

take timber touch tumbler thongs gentle fitness

Batman trounce rats twice duty trestle thing

Not all of the wonders of the world are to be

found on land. Deep sea trenches contain fantastic

landforms and creatures.

SELF ASSESSMENT

Rate the usefulness of this join.

☆ ☆☆ ☆☆☆

Want to explore this technique further?

Yes No Maybe

Date ___ / ___ / ___

You can write f with a slanted crossbar. You may find it easier to join from this f.

Using this f also lets you join f to e.

f fi fe

f f f fa fe fi fo fu fl fr ft

furry fiend feeble flea feed friendly flautist

The Dead Sea is so salty, fish can't survive in it.

The saltiness makes the water very buoyant. It's

tricky to swim in, but you can sit in it as

though you're sitting in a bean bag.

SELF ASSESSMENT

Rate the usefulness of this join.

☆ ☆☆ ☆☆☆

Want to explore this technique further?

Yes No Maybe

Date ___ /___ /___

Karen April

Try out some different ways you could join these capitals to the letter after them.

C

E

F

H

K

L

M

N

Q

R

Date ___ / ___ / ___

There are many versions of flourished capitals. They're used in text you want to look fancy – not when you need to write quickly.

Trace then copy these flourished capitals.

A B C D E F G H I J K L M

N O P Q R S T U V W X Y Z

Write your name and address using flourished capitals for the capital letters.

Write the names of some people you admire, using flourished capitals for the capital letters.

SELF ASSESSMENT

Circle your best example of each flourished capital.

Date ___ /___ /___

Try out some personalised versions of capital letters.

A ______ N ______
B ______ O ______
C ______ P ______
D ______ Q ______
E ______ R ______
F ______ S ______
G ______ T ______
H ______ U ______
I ______ V ______
J ______ W ______
K ______ X ______
L ______ Y ______
M ______ Z ______

Choose the versions you like best, and write your alphabet of personalised capitals here.

Developing your own style – Monograms

Date ___ / ___ / ___

Here are some sample monograms:

Try designing some monograms using your initials.

Redo your favourite one here:

Date ___ /___ /___

It's useful to have a signature that is distinctive. Signatures are used when signing letters and forms, and in many other places.

A signature doesn't have to be really fancy. Just your own ordinary handwriting will be hard for someone else to mimic.

Here are some example signatures.

Try out your own signature here. Remember – a signature should be easy to write, and easy to remember. The idea is for it to become automatic.

_______________________ _______________________

_______________________ _______________________

_______________________ _______________________

_______________________ _______________________

Write your favourite version of your signature here:

____

Developing your own style – Flourished alphabet

Date ___ / ___ / ___

When you print, lower-case letters can also be written in a flourished style.

Flourished letters are for when you have time to write slowly and want something to look fancy.

Trace then copy the flourished lower-case letters.

a b c d e f g h i j k l m

n o p q r s t u v w x y z

a b c d e f g h i j k l m

n o p q r s t u v w x y z

Write your name and address using flourished capitals and lower-case letters.

Date ___ / ___ / ___ **Developing your own style – Personalised lower-case letters**

Try designing your own flourished lower-case letters.

Remember – only use fancy letters when presentation is important, and when you're not in a hurry.

a

b

c

d

e

f

g

h

i

j

k

l

m

n

o

p

q

r

s

t

u

v

w

x

y

z

Choose your favourite version for each letter and write your personalised flourished alphabet here.

Date ___ /___ /___

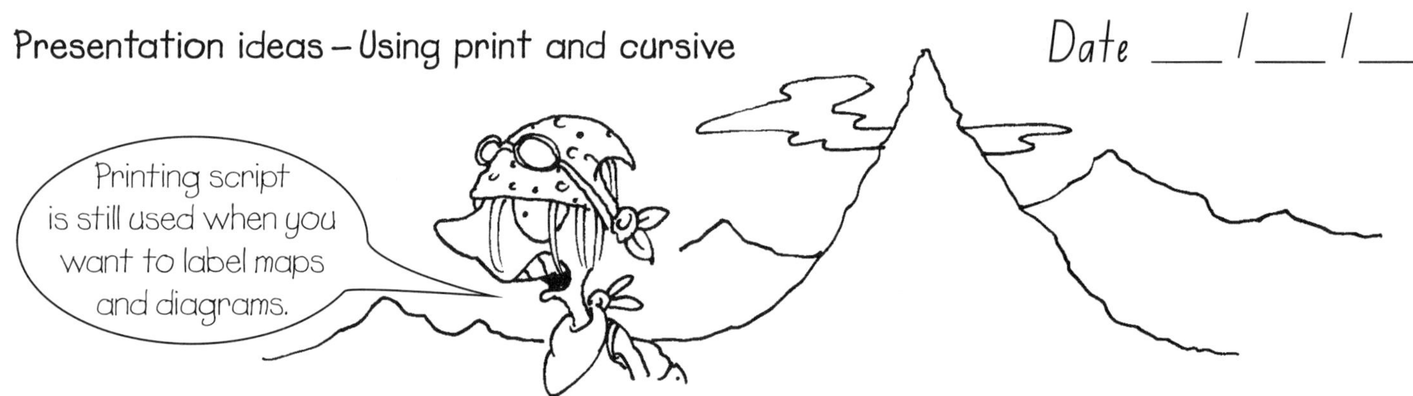

Label this diagram of the south route to the summit of Mt Everest.

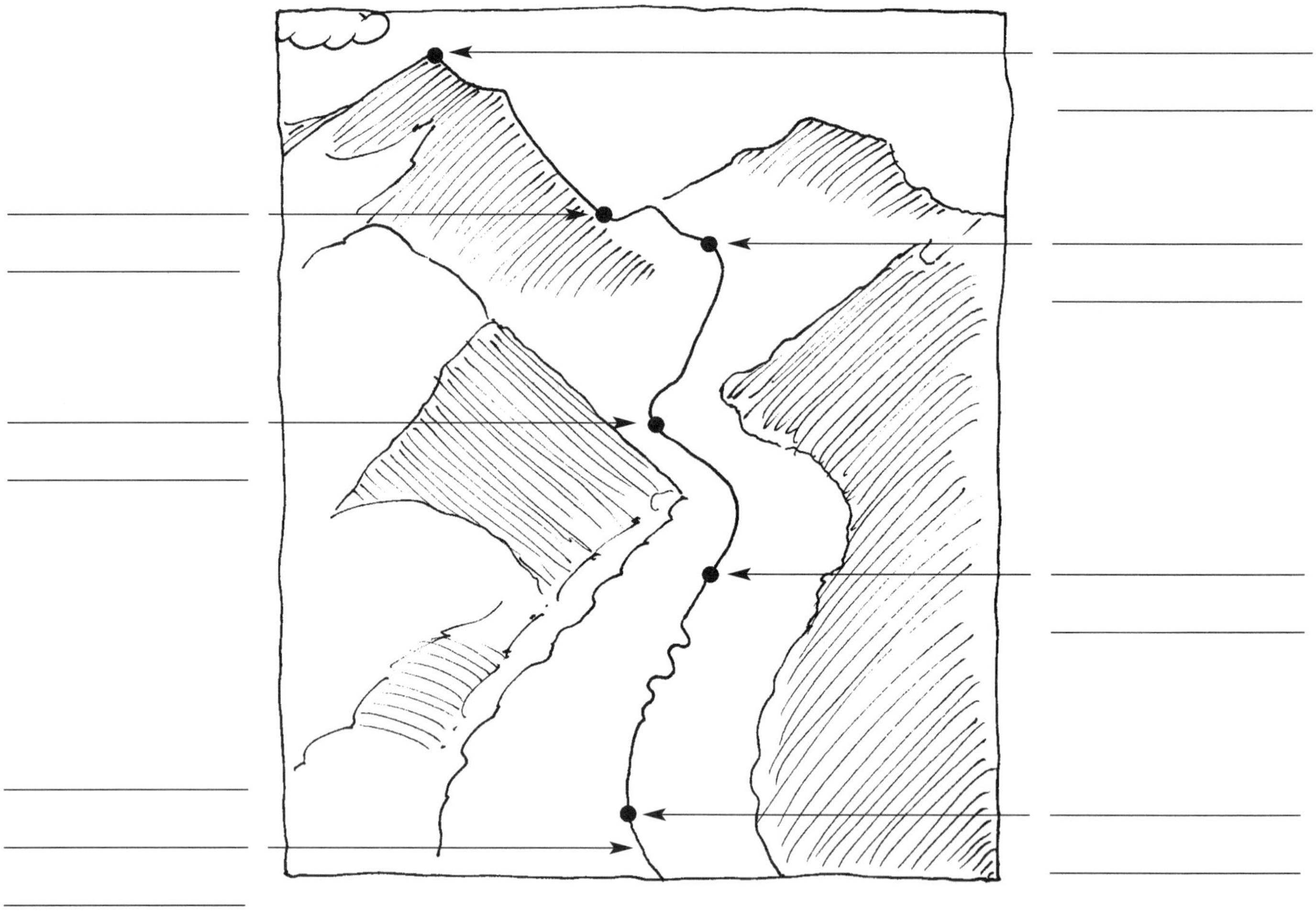

Base Camp (5,395 m)	Camp I (6,066 m)	Camp II (6,492 m)
Camp III (7,468 m)	Camp IV (7,925 m)	Summit (8,850 m)
Route to the summit		

SELF ASSESSMENT — Rate your printing script.

☆	☆ ☆	☆ ☆ ☆
Needs work	Monumental effort	Spectacular!

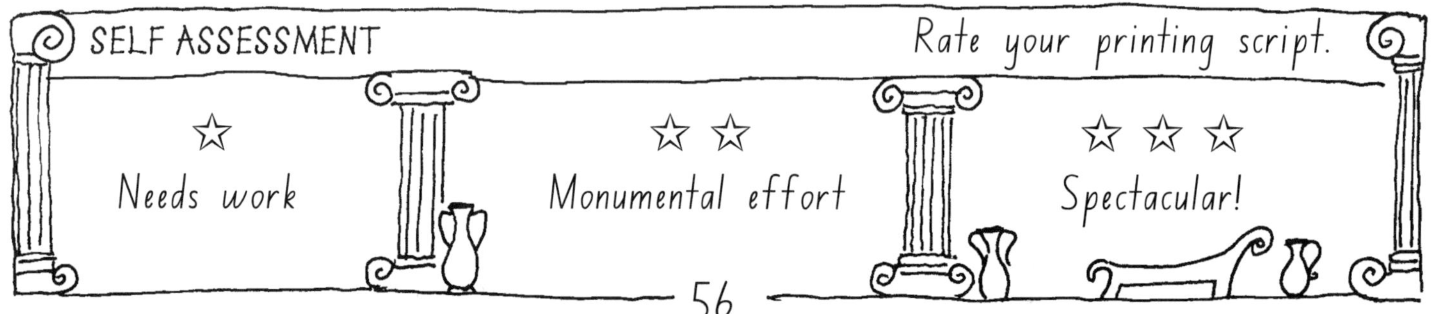

Date ___ / ___ / ___

Label this diagram of a mountaineer's equipment, using printing script.
Then write out the list of equipment in cursive.

clothing in layers	lightweight, flexible boots	gaiters	waterproof backpack
sun protection	sleeping mat	water bottle	helmet

Equipment list

Date ___ / ___ / ___

Fill in this form, using capitals.

Grand Canyon National Park Internal Aviation

FLIGHT REQUEST FORM

NAME: ______________________________

ADDRESS: ______________________________

____

PILOT LICENCE NO.: ______________________________

DAY, DATE AND TIME FLIGHT IS REQUESTED: ______________________________

____

PASSENGERS' NAMES:

1. ______________________________
2. ______________________________
3. ______________________________

CARGO ITEMS AND WEIGHTS:

1. ______________________ / ____ kg
2. ______________________ / ____ kg
3. ______________________ / ____ kg
4. ______________________ / ____ kg

REASON FOR FLIGHT: ______________________________

____

SIGNATURE: ______________________ DATE: ____________

NOTE TO TRIP ORGANISER: IF FLIGHT IS APPROVED, THE COMPLETED AND SIGNED FORM MUST BE AT THE HELIBASE BY FLIGHT TIME.

Date ___ / ___ / ___

You can use headings to add to the look of projects or assignments.

UNDERGROUND

Choose four of the titles below, and create a different style of heading for each.

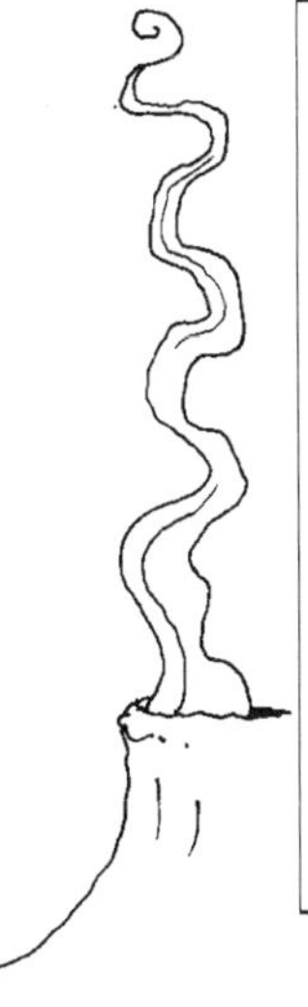

The Curse of the Mummy's Tomb
Leaning Tower Finally Topples!
How to Spot a Coelacanth
Thoughts of a Navel Fluff Collector
Why the Dead Sea is So Salty
Come to Stunning Keli Mutu!

Date ___ / ___ / ___

This is the element that has been repeated to create the border around this page

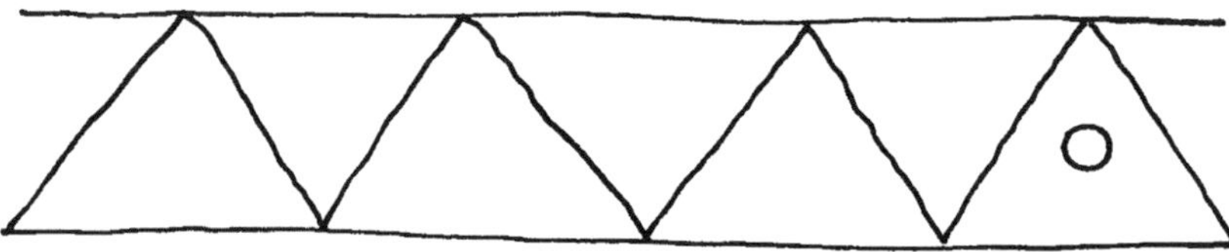

Design two border elements, then see how they each look in an extended section.

Date ___ /___ /___

Have a look at these sample business cards.

ALIKI'S POLAR EXPEDITION SUPPLIES AND HUSKY EMPORIUM

Aliki Garofalis, Licensed husky breeder

Pure-bred Siberian Huskies and Alaskan Malamutes.

Plus all the equipment you'll need for your trip to the Pole.

347 Byrd Drive, Scotthurst, Tasmania

www.huskiesRus.com

Jake Skyseeker

Hot Air Balloonist

Get a bird's eye view of the world!

Dawn flights a specialty – breakfast included.

The sky's the limit!

Ph 0405 222 007

Now choose two professions and design business cards for yourself.

Date ___ /___ /___

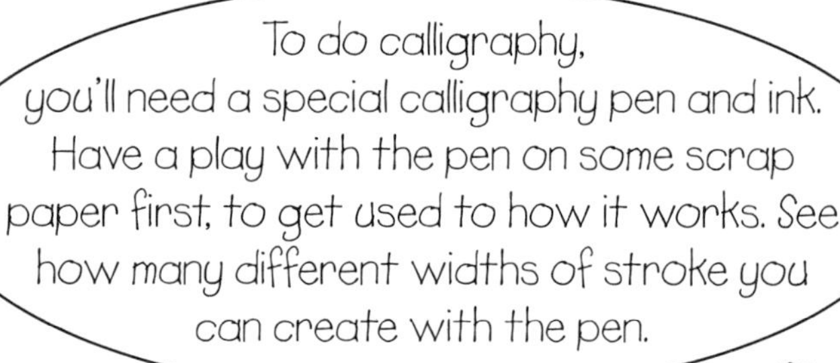

Try out these strokes, remembering to keep your pen at an angle of 45 degrees.

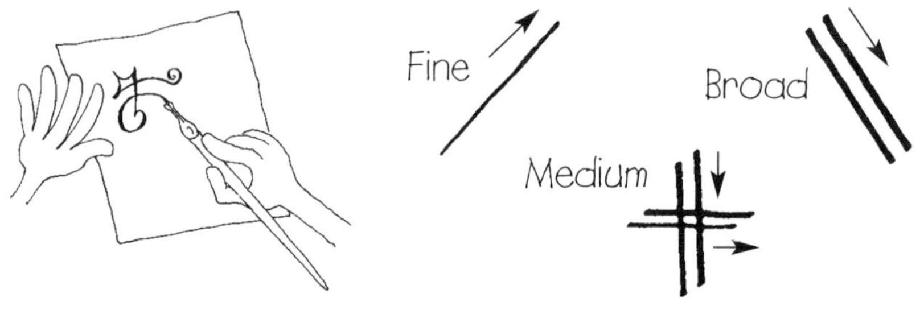

Copy these letters. The capitals are called uncials, and the lower-case version are half uncials.

A B C D E F G H I J K L M

N O P Q R S T U V W X Y Z

a b c d e f g h i j k l m

n o p q r s t u v w x y z

Date ___ / ___ / ___

Use your calligraphy pen and uncial script to address this envelope to a friend, and write your own name and address on the back.

Date ___ /___ /___

At the end of the year, collect autographs from the people in your class. An autograph can simply be a signature, or can include a funny message or rhyme.

Autographs